MIRACULOUS MIMI
the Micro Preemie

Holly Luky

Miraculous Mimi the Micro Preemie

Copyright © 2019 by Holly Luky

All rights reserved. No part of this publication may be reproduced, distributed, or transmitted in any form or by any means, including photocopying, recording, or other electronic or mechanical methods, without the prior written permission of the publisher or author, except in the case of brief quotations embodied in critical reviews and certain other noncommercial uses permitted by copyright law. For information, contact the author.

ISBN-13: 978-0-578-46178-6
ISBN-10: 0-578-46178-1

Printed in the United States of America

MIRACULOUS MIMI
the Micro Preemie

Written by **Holly Luky**

Illustrations by Something of a Dandy

Even before she was born, Mimi's parents knew she was **EXTRAORDINARY.** You see, they had prayed for Mimi for a long time.

When they found out Mimi was coming, they were delighted!
Especially Bella, who was excited to have a baby sister.

Together, Bella and her parents read to Mimi every night.

And Bella picked out clothes that she wanted to save for her new sister.

Mama's belly grew into a small bump, which Bella thought was beautiful. It was all very exciting.

One warm summer day, Mama woke up worried. Bella and her parents rushed off to the hospital to make sure everything was okay with Mimi.

The doctors were very nice, and they got to watch Mimi in Mama's belly. Though Mama and Dada were still worried, they prayed that Mimi would be just fine.

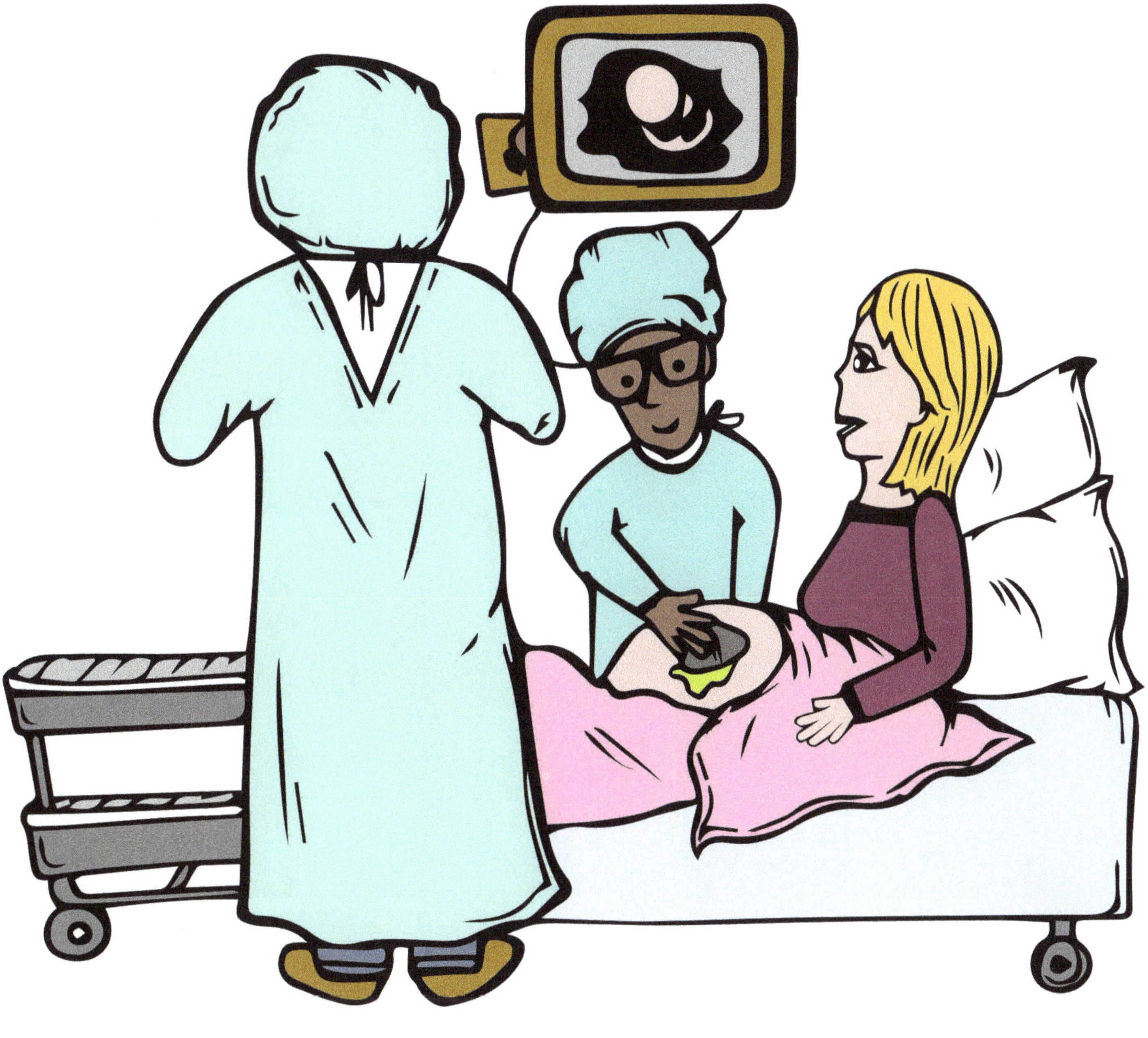

The nurses took good care of Mama, Mimi, and Bella.
The nurses brought special gifts for Bella.

Even Nana, Papa, Auntie, and cousins all got to visit!
Mama was happy they could all be together.

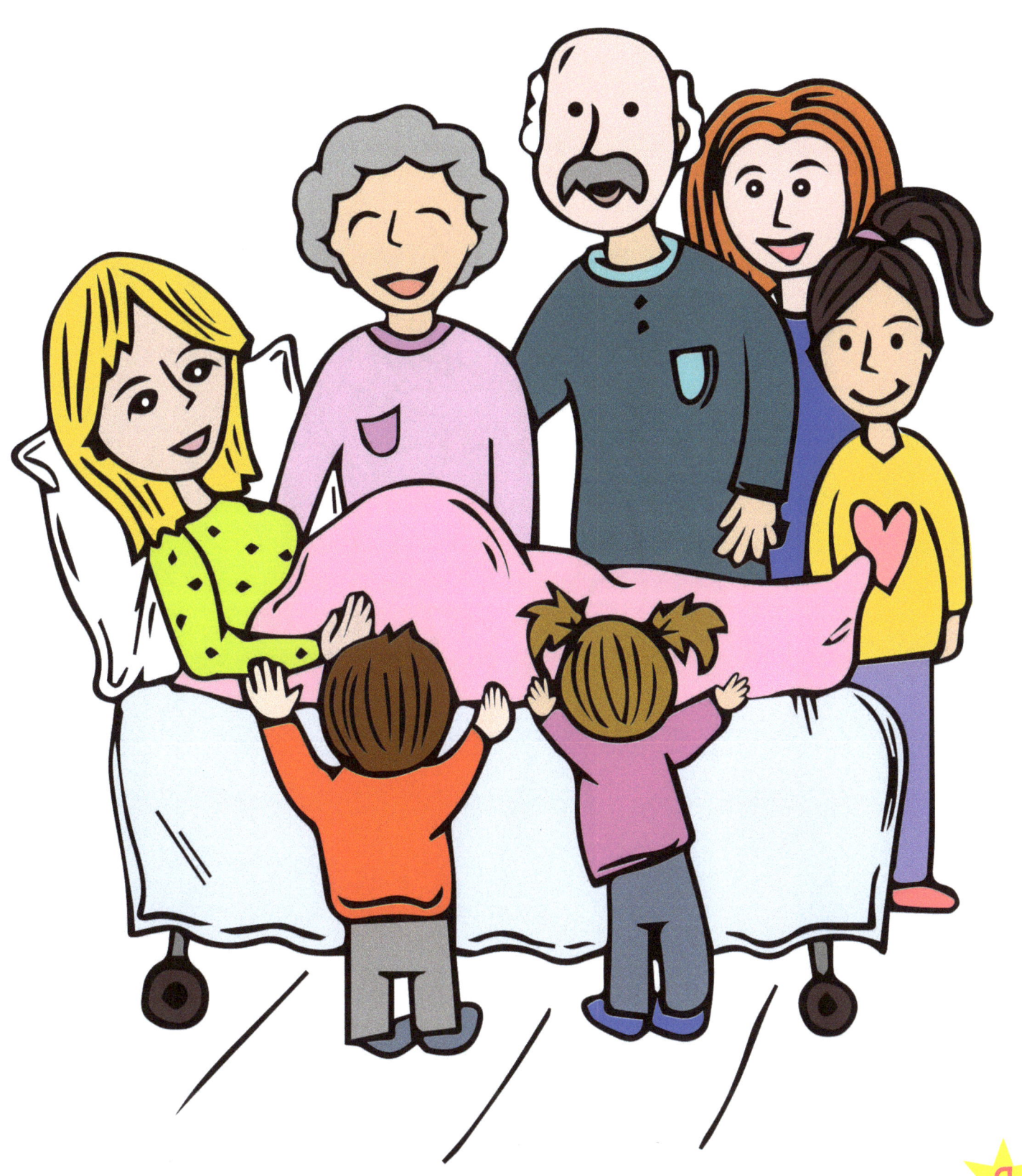

One evening, things got very exciting.
Mama knew this meant Mimi was coming!
With a lot of help from doctors and nurses,
Mimi was born!

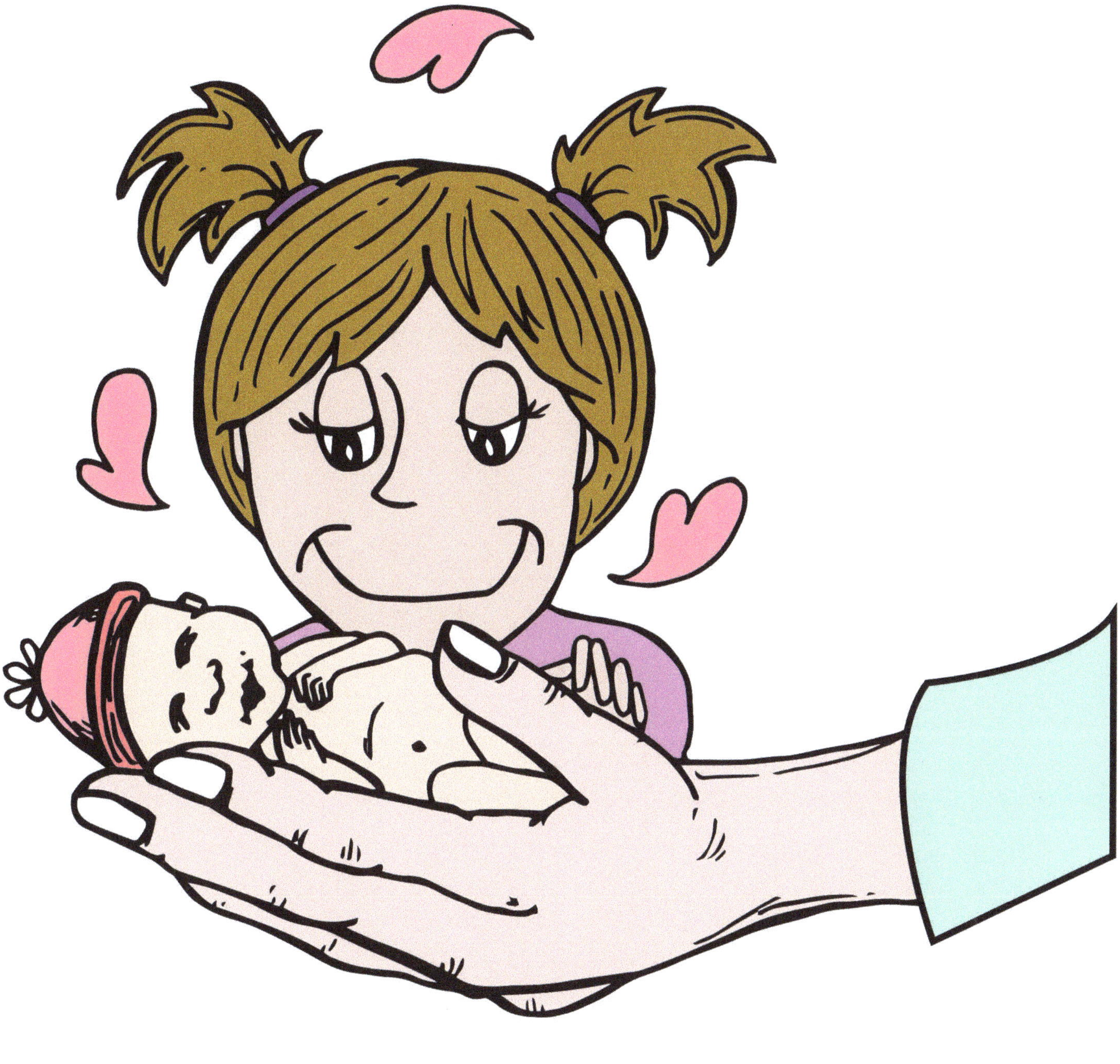

But Mimi was born very early and was very tiny.
Bella thought she was beautiful.

Mama explained that because she was born so early, Mimi was called a "micro preemie." Mama said Mimi had to live in a special place called the NICU for a little while.

Mimi had a lot of attention in the NICU.
She especially liked having her nurses' attention.

Mama and Dada visited Mimi every day.
They held her tiny hands.

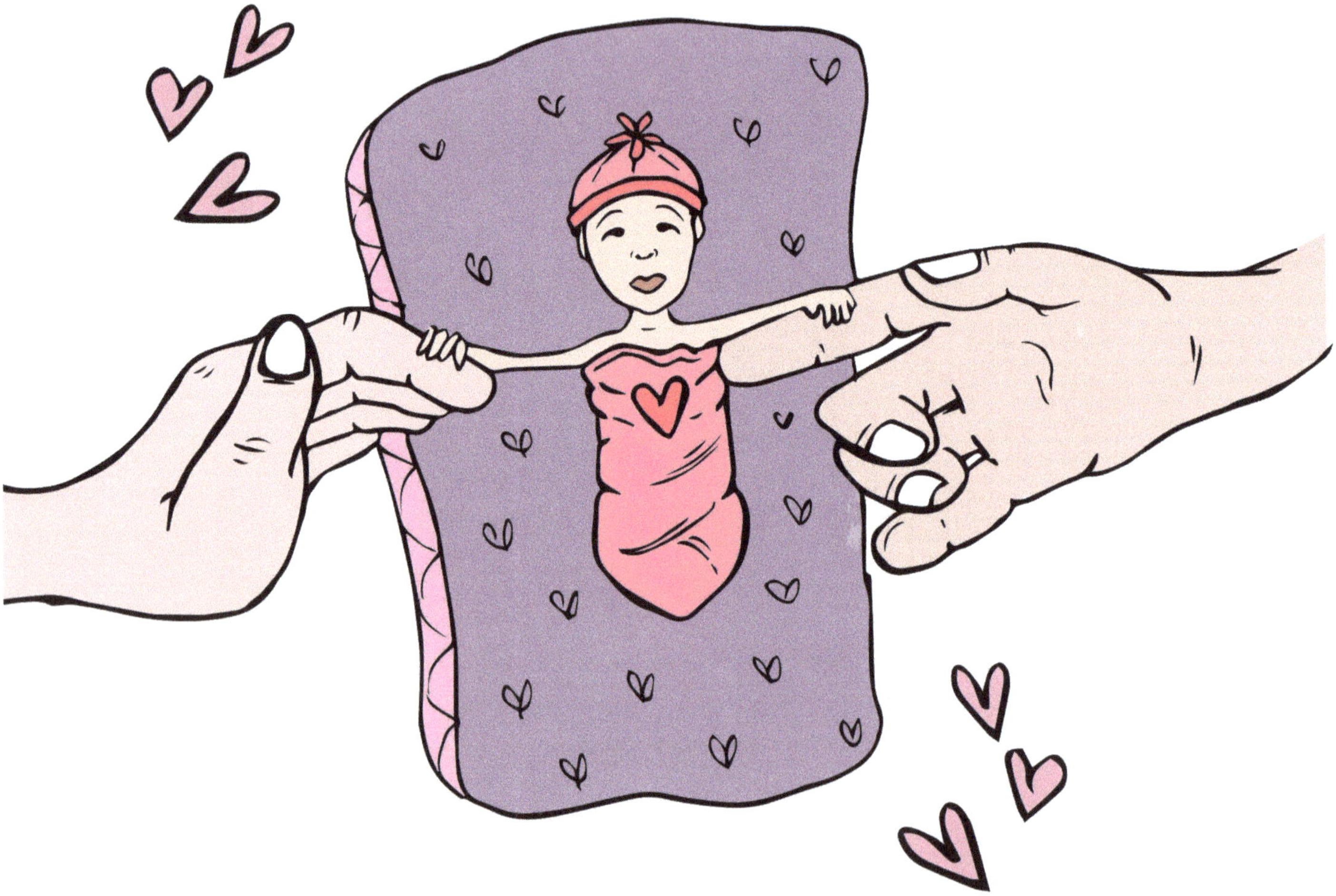

Mama and Dada snuggled Mimi close to their chests so she could hear their hearts beat. She was nice and warm.

While in the NICU, Mimi grew a little bit each day. This was a very important time for Mimi, because while most babies grow inside their mama's belly, Mimi grew up inside the NICU. Mimi's doctors and nurses took great care of her.

With each day,
Mimi grew stronger.

Mama and Dada would come home and tell Bella all about Mimi's adventures in the NICU. It was hard for Bella to not have her sister at home with her. It was hard for Mama and Dada, too.

As Mimi began to grow bigger, Mama and Dada were able to take care of her in the NICU. Mimi loved bath time! But most of all, she loved being held.

Mimi made a lot of noise inside the NICU. Everyone knew who Mimi was. She had special machines that would beep if she moved too much. She moved a lot!
So she caused a lot of beeping.

Mimi wanted to be held a lot. This made everyone smile because it meant that soon Mimi would be strong enough to come home.

On one particularly special day, Bella woke up to see the leaves changing outside. She was excited. She knew that when the leaves began to change, her baby sister would soon be coming home.

Sure enough, when Mama and Dada went into the NICU that day, the doctors had wonderful news to share.

Mimi was ready to come home!

Together, Mama, Dada and Bella got dressed up in their nicest outfits. They had prayed for this day to come for many months.

When they arrived at the NICU, Mimi was surrounded by presents from her nurses. This made Bella smile, too.

Mimi's nurses were sad to see her leave the NICU, but they loved seeing Bella and Mimi finally together. It was all very special. As they left the hospital together, Bella held Mimi's tiny hand.

Mimi loved being home with her family.
Bella loved that her sister was home.

Mimi's family knew she was a miracle. She was their miracle. She was, after all, miraculous Mimi, their micro preemie.

About the Author

Holly Luky is a writer who resides in the mountains of beautiful Northern Arizona with two inspiring little girls, a husband and small homestead of animals. When not absorbed in a new project, she enjoys cooking, baking, reading, and spending time in nature.

www.ingramcontent.com/pod-product-compliance
Lightning Source LLC
Chambersburg PA
CBHW061751290426

44108CB00028B/2955